بِسْمِ اللهِ

الرَّحْمٰنِ

الرَّحِيْمِ

bismillah

ar-Rahman

ar-Raheem

*(1:1) In the name of Allah,
the Most Merciful,
the Ever Merciful*

Excerpt taken from <u>Tafsir Ibn Kathir (section 1.1)</u>:

"Imam Ahmad recorded in his <u>Musnad,</u> that a person who was riding behind the Prophet [PBUH] said,
'The Prophet's animal tripped, so I said, "Cursed Shaytan."

The Prophet said,

لَا تَقُلْ: تَعِسَ الشَّيْطَانُ، فَإِنَّكَ إِذَا قُلْتَ: تَعِسَ الشَّيْطَانُ، تَعَاظَمَ وَقَالَ: «بِقُوَّتِي صَرَعْتُهُ، وَإِذَا قُلْتَ: بِاسْمِ اللهِ تَصَاغَرَ حَتَى يَصِيرَ مِثْلَ الذُّبَابِ»

*(Do not say, 'Cursed Shaytan,' for if you say these words,
Satan becomes arrogant and says,
'With my strength I made him fall.'
When you say, 'Bismillah,' Satan will become as small as a fly.)*

Further, An-Nasa'i recorded in his book <u>Al-Yawm wal-Laylah,</u> and also Ibn Marduwyah in his <u>Tafsir</u> that Usamah bin `Umayr said, "I was riding behind the Prophet..." and he mentioned the rest of the above Hadith.

The Prophet said in this narration,

لَا تَقُلْ هَكَذَا فَإِنَّهُ يَتَعَاظَمُ حَتَّى يَكُونَ كَالْبَيْتِ، وَلَكِنْ قُلْ: بِسْمِ اللهِ، فَإِنَّهُ يَصْغَرُ حَتَّى يَكُونَ كَالذُّبَابَة

*(Do not say these words, because then Satan becomes larger;
as large as a house. Rather, say, 'Bismillah,' because Satan then
becomes as small as a fly.)*

This is the blessing of reciting Bismillah...
Basmalah (reciting Bismillah) is recommended
before starting any action or deed."

as-selamu alaikum
(may peace be upon you)!
May Allah (S.W.T.) guide us each towards
fruitful & meaningful knowledge! Ameen!

Primary Source:

for most frequent words information
(original first three pages from chart printed at the
end of this book)
**Source website no longer online
but here's a direct link to the document:**
http://quran.ilmsummit.org/projects/quran/QuranWordFrequency.pdf

* According to the original source, there are **77,429** words in the
Qur'an reduced to **4,845** after removing duplicates and conjugations.
There are many different "words in Qur'an" totals, depending on the
calculation method and the definition of what constitutes a "word."
This book highlights 60 words translated into English
(not necessarily considered words in Arabic).

Secondary Source:

for Surah names in Arabic and English, # of aya,
revelation location, aya translation, and notes:
Al-Quran (2014): al-quran.info/

Surah Yunus [AS] 10:57-

يا أَيُّهَا النَّاسُ قَد جاءَتكُم مَوعِظَةٌ مِن رَبِّكُم وَشِفاءٌ لِما فِي الصُّدورِ وَهُدًى وَرَحمَةٌ لِلمُؤمِنينَ

"O mankind! There has certainly come to you an advice from your Lord, and a cure for what is in the breasts, and a guidance and mercy for the faithful."

Simple Tashkeel (sound rules) for Pronunciation & Reading:

fat-ha	◌َ	Adds "a" sound after a letter: *Sounds like "a" in "fat cat"*	Shape at End of Word	◌ً *Sounds like "-an"*
kes-ra	◌ِ	Adds "ee" sound after a letter: *Sounds like "ee" in "green"*	Shape at End of Word	◌ٍ *Sounds like "-een"*
dam-ma	◌ُ	Adds "oo" sound after a letter: *Sounds like "oo" in "moon"*	Shape at End of Word	◌ٌ *Sounds like "-oon"*
shad-da	◌ّ	**Makes the letter double its sound**		*Acts like the "m" sound in "sum-mer"*
sa-koon	◌ْ	**Makes the letter stop on its sound**		*Acts like not adding any vowel:* مِنْ *is "meen"*
hamza	ء	**Makes a sound like when you try to clear your throat**		*Limits the "a" sound for Alif*

MY PROGRESS CHART for the first half!

1		2		3		4		5		6	
English:		English:		English:		English:		English:		English:	
Arabic:		Arabic:		Arabic:		Arabic:		Arabic:		Arabic:	
Aya:		Aya:		Aya:		Aya:		Aya:		Aya:	

7		8		9		10		11		12	
English:		English:		English:		English:		English:		English:	
Arabic:		Arabic:		Arabic:		Arabic:		Arabic:		Arabic:	
Aya:		Aya:		Aya:		Aya:		Aya:		Aya:	

13		14		15		16		17		18	
English:		English:		English:		English:		English:		English:	
Arabic:		Arabic:		Arabic:		Arabic:		Arabic:		Arabic:	
Aya:		Aya:		Aya:		Aya:		Aya:		Aya:	

19		20		21		22		23		24	
English:		English:		English:		English:		English:		English:	
Arabic:		Arabic:		Arabic:		Arabic:		Arabic:		Arabic:	
Aya:		Aya:		Aya:		Aya:		Aya:		Aya:	

25		26		27		28		29		30	
English:		English:		English:		English:		English:		English:	
Arabic:		Arabic:		Arabic:		Arabic:		Arabic:		Arabic:	
Aya:		Aya:		Aya:		Aya:		Aya:		Aya:	

Some Study Ideas:

→ **Highlight each word in the aya on each flashcard**

→ **Memorize 1 page (6 words) each week**
- o Finish in 10 weeks, in shaa Allah!

→ **Work on one flashcard a week, a day, a month**
- o Just regularly do it!

→ **Practice (out loud or in your head) throughout the day**

→ **Keep track of your progress with regular check-ins!**

→ **Copy one flashcard a day, reflect on it & carry it around**

→ **CHALLENGE 1:**
- o Open any page of the Qur'an & find the words you know!

→ **CHALLENGE 2:**
- o Learn together, in shaa Allah!
  - ▪ Print out a copy of this book (2-sided, flip on long edge) and bring it to the mosque, Islamic study group, school, a family gathering, a friend's house, the mall, anywhere!

PS: IF YOU FIND ANY ERROR THAT NEEDS CORRECTING, PLEASE GET IN TOUCH: <u>READANDRECITE.ORG</u>

2 الله	**1** مِنْ
4 فِي	**3** لَا
6 قُلْ	**5** إِنَّ

Allah (2)
(ALLAH)
Number of occurrences in Qur'an: 2,699

Surah al-Ikhlas 112:2-

اللَّهُ الصَّمَدُ

"Allah-us-Samad [The Self-Sufficient Master, Whom all creatures need, He neither eats nor drinks]"

from, of (1)
(MEEN)
Number of occurrences in Qur'an: 3,226

Surah al-Falaq 113:2-

مِنْ شَرِّ مَا خَلَقَ

"From the evil of that which He has created;"

in (4)
(FEE)
Number of occurrences in Qur'an: 1,701

Surah at-Tur 52:3-

فِي رَقٍّ مَنْشُورٍ

"In parchment unrolled"

no, not (3)
(LA)
Number of occurrences in Qur'an: 2.323

Surah al-Qiyamah 75:11-

كَلَّا لَا وَزَرَ

"No! There is no refuge!"

to say (6)
(QUL)
Number of occurrences in Qur'an: 1,618

Surah al-Qiyamah 75:27-

وَقِيلَ مَنْ رَاقٍ

"And it will be said: 'Who can cure him and save him from death?'"

indeed (5)
(EENA)
Number of occurrences in Qur'an: 1,682

Surah al-Waqi'ah 56:66-

إِنَّا لَمُغْرَمُونَ

(Saying): "We are indeed Mughramun [i.e. ruined or lost the money without any profit or punished of all that we spent for cultivation, etc]." see Tafsir Al-Qurtubi, Vol 17, pg 219

8 عَلَى	7 اَلَّذِى
10 كَانَ	9 لَ
12 رَبٌّ	11 مَا

on  8

('ALA)

Number of occurrences in Qur'an: 1,445

Surah al-Muddaththir 74:30-

عَلَيْهَا تِسْعَةَ عَشَرَ

"Over it are nineteen [angels as guardians and keepers of Hell]"

who, which, that  7

(A'LADHEE)

Number of occurrences in Qur'an: 1,465

Surah ash-Sharh 94:3-

الَّذِي أَنقَضَ ظَهْرَكَ

"Which weighed down your back?"

to be 10

(KANA)

Number of occurrences in Qur'an: 1,358

Surah as-Saffat 37:167-

كَلَّا لا وَزَرَ

"And indeed [Arab pagans] used to say;"

for 9

(LA)

Number of occurrences in Qur'an: 1,407

Surah at-Tur 52:8-

مَا لَهُ مِن دَافِعٍ

"There is none that can avert it;"

Lord 12

(RAAB)

Number of occurrences in Qur'an: 975

Surah al-Muddaththir 74:3-

وَرَبَّكَ فَكَبِّرْ

"And your Lord (Allah) magnify!'"

what 11

(MA)

Number of occurrences in Qur'an: 1,174

Surah al-Haqqah 69:2-

مَا الْحَاقَّةُ

"What is the reality?"

14	13
بِ	مَنْ
16	15
إِنْ	إِلَى
18	17
أَنْ	إِلَّا

with, by (14)

(BEE)

Number of occurrences in Qur'an: 819

Surah Ta Ha 20:31-

اشْدُدْ بِهِ أَزْرِي

"Increase my strength with him [Musa (AS) making du'a referring to Harun (AS)]"

who (13)

(MAN)

Number of occurrences in Qur'an: 824

Surah an-Naazi'at 79:37-

فَأَمَّا مَن طَغَىٰ

"Then, for him who Tagha [transgressed all bounds in disbelief, oppression and evil deeds of disobedience to Allah]."

not (16)

(EEN)

Number of occurrences in Qur'an: 694

Surah Fatir 35:23-

إِنْ أَنتَ إِلَّا نَذِيرٌ

"You (O Muhammad PBUH) are only a warner [i.e. your duty is to convey Allah's Message to mankind but the guidance is in Allah's Hand]."

to, toward, until (15)

(EEL-AA)

Number of occurrences in Qur'an: 742

Surah al-Mursalat 77:22-

إِلَىٰ قَدَرٍ مَّعْلُومٍ

"Until a known period (determined by gestation)?"

that, to (18)

('AN)

Number of occurrences in Qur'an: 613

Surah al-Alaq 96:7-

أَن رَّآهُ اسْتَغْنَىٰ

"Because he considers himself self-sufficient"

except (17)

(EEL-LA)

Number of occurrences in Qur'an: 664

Surah al-Ma'arij 70:22-

إِلَّا الْمُصَلِّينَ

"Except those devoted to salat [prayers]"

20	19
ذَٰلِكَ	عَامَنَ

22	21
هُوَ	عَنْ

24	23
إِذَا	ٱلْأَرْضُ

that (20)

(DHALEEKA)

Number of occurrences in Qur'an: 479

Surah al-Qalam 68:13-

"Cruel, after all that baseborn [born of illegitimate birth]"

to believe (19)

('AMANA)

Number of occurrences in Qur'an: 537

Surah al-'Inshiqaq 84:20-

"What is the matter with them, that they believe not?"

he (22)

(HOOWA)

Number of occurrences in Qur'an: 464

Surah 'Abasa 80:9-

"And he is afraid [of Allah and His punishment]"

from / about (21)

('AN)

Number of occurrences in Qur'an: 465

Surah al-Muddaththir 74:41-

"About al-mujrimun [(polytheists, criminals, disbelievers, etc), (And they will say to them)]:"

when (24)

(EEDHĀ)

Number of occurrences in Qur'an: 423

Surah al-'Alaq 96:10-

"A slave [Muhammad PBUH] when he prays?"

the earth; land (23)

(AL-ARD)

Number of occurrences in Qur'an: 461

Surah al-Inshiqaq 84:3-

"And when the earth is stretched forth,"

26	25
يَوْمٌ	قَدْ

28	27
الْآيَةِ	قَوْمٌ

30	29
هُمْ	عَلَمٌ

day (26)

(YAWM)

Number of occurrences in Qur'an: 405

Surah al-Mutaffifin 83:5-

لِيَوْمٍ عَظِيمٍ

"On a Great Day,"

indeed (25)

(QAD)

Number of occurrences in Qur'an: 406

Surah ash-Shams 91:10-

وَقَدْ خَابَ مَن دَسَّاهَا

"And indeed he fails who corrupts his own self [i.e. disobeys what Allah has ordered by rejecting the True faith of Islamic Monotheism or by following polytheism, etc. or by doing every kind of evil wicked deeds]"

sign, revelation (28)

(AL-AYA[T])

Number of occurrences in Qur'an: 382

Surah an-Naazi'at 79:20-

فَأَرَاهُ الْآيَةَ الْكُبْرَىٰ

"Then [Musa (AS)] showed him the great sign [miracles]."

people (27)

(QAWM)

Number of occurrences in Qur'an: 383

Surah al-Qamar 54:33-

كَذَّبَتْ قَوْمُ لُوطٍ بِالنُّذُرِ

"The people of Lut (AS) belied the warnings."

they (30)

(HUM)

Number of occurrences in Qur'an: 370

Surah al-Ma'un 170:6-

الَّذِينَ هُمْ يُرَاءُونَ

"They who do good deeds only to be seen [of men]"

knowledge (29)

('ALEEMA)

Number of occurrences in Qur'an: 382

Surah an-Naba' 78:4-

كَلَّا سَيَعْلَمُونَ

"Nay! They will come to know!"

MY PROGRESS CHART for the second half!

31		32		33		34		35		36	
English:		English:		English:		English:		English:		English:	
Arabic:		Arabic:		Arabic:		Arabic:		Arabic:		Arabic:	
Aya:		Aya:		Aya:		Aya:		Aya:		Aya:	

37		38		39		40		41		42	
English:		English:		English:		English:		English:		English:	
Arabic:		Arabic:		Arabic:		Arabic:		Arabic:		Arabic:	
Aya:		Aya:		Aya:		Aya:		Aya:		Aya:	

43		44		45		46		47		48	
English:		English:		English:		English:		English:		English:	
Arabic:		Arabic:		Arabic:		Arabic:		Arabic:		Arabic:	
Aya:		Aya:		Aya:		Aya:		Aya:		Aya:	

49		50		51		52		53		54	
English:		English:		English:		English:		English:		English:	
Arabic:		Arabic:		Arabic:		Arabic:		Arabic:		Arabic:	
Aya:		Aya:		Aya:		Aya:		Aya:		Aya:	

55		56		57		58		59		60	
English:		English:		English:		English:		English:		English:	
Arabic:		Arabic:		Arabic:		Arabic:		Arabic:		Arabic:	
Aya:		Aya:		Aya:		Aya:		Aya:		Aya:	

Surah al-Qamar (The Moon) 54-

إِنَّا نَحْنُ نَزَّلْنَا الذِّكْرَ وَإِنَّا لَهُ لَحَافِظُونَ ٩

*"Indeed We have sent down the Reminder [The Qur'an]
and indeed We will preserve it."*

Surah al-Isra (The Night Journey) 17-

إِنَّ هٰذَا الْقُرآنَ يَهدي لِلَّتي هِيَ أَقْوَمُ وَيُبَشِّرُ الْمُؤمِنينَ ٩ الَّذينَ يَعمَلونَ الصّالِحاتِ أَنَّ لَهُم أَجْرًا كَبيرًا

*"Indeed this Qurʾān guides to what is most upright,
and gives the good news to the faithful who do righteous deeds
that there is a great reward for them."*

...

وَنُنَزِّلُ مِنَ الْقُرآنِ ما هُوَ شِفاءٌ وَرَحْمَةٌ لِلمُؤمِنينَ ٨٢ وَلا يَزيدُ الظّالِمينَ إِلّا خَسارًا

*"We send down in the Qurʾān that which is a cure and mercy for the
faithful; and it increases the wrongdoers only in loss."*

Surah al-Nahl (The Bee) 16-

وَما أَنزَلنا عَلَيكَ الكِتابَ إِلّا لِتُبَيِّنَ لَهُمُ الَّذي اخْتَلَفوا ٦٤ فيهِ وَهُدًى وَرَحْمَةً لِقَومٍ يُؤمِنونَ

*"We did not send down the Book to you except [for the purpose]
that you may clarify for them what they differ about,
and as a guidance and mercy for a people who have faith."*

32	31
كُلّ	أَنَّ
34	33
ثُمَّ	لَمْ
36	35
رَسُول	جَعَلَ

everyone  32

(KOOL)

Number of occurrences in Qur'an: 359

Surah ar-Rahman 55:26-

كُلُّ مَنْ عَلَيْهَا فَانٍ

*"Whatsoever is on it [the earth]
will perish"*

that  31

(AN-NA)

Number of occurrences in Qur'an: 366

Surah al-Qiyamah 75:28-

وَظَنَّ أَنَّهُ الْفِرَاقُ

*"And he [the dying person]
will conclude that it was
[the time] of departing [death];"*

then  34

(THOOMMA)

Number of occurrences in Qur'an: 341

Surah al-Muddaththir 74:21-

ثُمَّ نَظَرَ

"Then he thought;"

not  33

(LAM)

Number of occurrences in Qur'an: 348

Surah al-Ikhlas 112:3-

لَمْ يَلِدْ وَلَمْ يُولَدْ

*"He begets not
nor was he begotten"*

the messengers (of Allah SWT)  36

(RASOOL)

Number of occurrences in Qur'an: 332

Surah al-Mursalat 77:11-

وَإِذَا الرُّسُلُ أُقِّتَتْ

*"And when the messengers are
gathered to their time appointed;"*

to make  35

(JA'ALA)

Number of occurrences in Qur'an: 340

Surah al-Alaq 87:5-

فَجَعَلَهُ غُثَاءً أَحْوَىٰ

"And then makes it dark stubble"

38	37
سَمَآء	عَذَاب
40	39
كَفَر	نَفْس
42	41
أَوْ	شَيْء

sky (38)

(SAMA'A)

Number of occurrences in Qur'an: 310

Surah at-Tariq 86:1-

وَٱلسَّمَآءِ وَٱلطَّارِقِ

"By the [heavens] and At-Tariq (the night corner, i.e. the bright star);"

punishment (37)

('ADAAB)

Number of occurrences in Qur'an: 322

Surah al-Qamar 54:39-

فَذُوقُوا۟ عَذَابِى وَنُذُرِ

"Then taste you My Torment and My Warnings"

to disbelieve (40)

(KAFAR)

Number of occurrences in Qur'an: 289

Surah al-Ghashiyah 88:23-

إِلَّا مَنْ تَوَلَّىٰ وَكَفَرَ

"Save the one who turns away and disbelieves"

self, soul, person, mind (39)

(NAFS)

Number of occurrences in Qur'an: 295

Surah ash-Shams 91:7-

وَنَفْسٍ وَمَا سَوَّاهَا

"And by Nafs and Him Who perfected him in proportion;"

or (42)

(OW) LIKE 'OW, THAT HURTS'

Number of occurrences in Qur'an: 280

Surah al-Mursalat 77:6-

عُذْرًا أَوْ نُذْرًا

"To cut off all excuses or to warn;"

thing (41)

(SHAY')

Number of occurrences in Qur'an: 283

Surah al-'Abasa 80:18-

مِنْ أَيِّ شَيْءٍ خَلَقَهُ

"From what thing did He create him?"

43 جَآءَ	44 عَمِلَ
45 لَوْ	46 هٰذَا
47 اَتَى	48 رَءَا

to do, to work 44

('AMEELA)

Number of occurrences in Qur'an: 276

Surah al-Hijr 15:93-

عَمَّا كَانُوا۟ يَعْمَلُونَ

"For all that they used to do"

to come, arrive 43

(JA'A')

Number of occurrences in Qur'an: 278

Surah 'Abasa 80:2-

أَن جَآءَهُ ٱلْأَعْمَىٰ

"Because there came to him the blind man"

this 46

(HADH-A)

Number of occurrences in Qur'an: 274

Surah al-Mursalat 77:35-

هَٰذَا يَوْمُ لَا يَنطِقُونَ

"This is a Day when they shall not speak (during some part of it)."

if 45

(LOW) LIKE 'L+OW, THAT HURTS'

Number of occurrences in Qur'an: 276

Surah al-Qiyamah 75:15

وَلَوْ أَلْقَىٰ مَعَاذِيرَهُ

"Though he may put forward his excuses [to cover his evil deeds]"

to see 48

(RA'A)

Number of occurrences in Qur'an: 271

Surah al-Ma'arij 70:7-

وَنَرَاهُ قَرِيبًا

"But We see it [quite] near"

to give, yield 47

(AATA)

Number of occurrences in Qur'an: 271

Surah al-Baqara 2:269-

يُؤْتِي الْحِكْمَةَ مَن يَشَاءُ

"Wisdom is given to whomever He wills..."

50 أَتَى	49 بَيْن
52 الْحَقّ	51 كُتِب
54 النَّاس	53 قَبْل

to come, to bring 50

(AATA)

Number of occurrences in Qur'an: 264

Surah al-Muddathir 74:47-

حَتَّىٰٓ أَتَىٰنَا ٱلْيَقِينُ

*"Until there came to us
[the death] that is certain."*

between them 49

(BAYN)

Number of occurrences in Qur'an: 266

Surah ar-Rahman 55:20-

بَيْنَهُمَا بَرْزَخٌ لَّا يَبْغِيَانِ

*"Between them is a barrier which
none of them can transgress"*

The Truth 52

(AL-HAQQ)

Number of occurrences in Qur'an: 247

Surah al-Mutaffifin 83:20-

كِتَٰبٌ مَّرْقُومٌ

*"A register inscribed
[It is a written record]"*

book 51

(KEETAB)

Number of occurrences in Qur'an: 260

Surah al-Haqqah 69:51-

كِتَٰبٌ مَّرْقُومٌ

*"And verily, it [this Qur'an] is an
absolute truth with certainty"*

mankind 54

(AN-NAAS)

Number of occurrences in Qur'an: 241

Surah an-Nas 114:2-

مَلِكِ ٱلنَّاسِ

"The King of mankind"

before 53

(QABL)

Number of occurrences in Qur'an: 242

Surah al-Waqi'ah 56:45-

إِنَّهُمْ كَانُوا۟ قَبْلَ ذَٰلِكَ مُتْرَفِينَ

*"Verily, before that,
they indulged in luxury"*

56	55
شَاءَ	إِذْ

58	57
الْمُؤْمِنُونَ	أُولَٰئِكَ

60	59
عِنْدَ	بَعْدُ

to will, to wish  56

(SHA'A)

Number of occurrences in Qur'an: 236

Surah 'Abasa 80:12-

فَمَنْ شَاءَ ذَكَرَهُ

*"So whoever wills,
let him pay attention to it."*

when  55

('EEDH)

Number of occurrences in Qur'an: 239

Surah ash-Shams 91:12-

إِذِ ٱنۢبَعَثَ أَشْقَٰلَهَا

*"When the most wicked man among
them went forth (to kill the she-
camel)."*

the believers  58

(AL MU'MEENOON)

Number of occurrences in Qur'an: 202

Surah al-Mu'minun 23:1-

قَدْ أَفْلَحَ الْمُؤْمِنُونَ

*"Successful indeed
are the believers."*

those  57

('OOLA'EEKA)

Number of occurrences in Qur'an: 208

Surah al-Waqi'ah 56:11-

أُولَٰئِكَ الْمُقَرَّبُونَ

*"[Those] will be those nearest to
Allah."*

near  60

('AYND)

Number of occurrences in Qur'an: 197

Surah al-Najm 53:14-

عِندَ سِدْرَةِ ٱلْمُنتَهَىٰ

*"Near Sidrat-ul-Muntaha
[lote tree of the utmost boundary]"*

after  59

(B'AYD)

Number of occurrences in Qur'an: 199

Surah Al-Muddaththir 74:15-

ثُمَّ يَطْمَعُ أَنْ أَزِيدَ

*"After all that, he desires
that I should give (yet) more;"*

Qur'an Word Frequency

Version 3.0

The purpose of this document is to help Muslims understand the language of the Qur'an & build their Qur'anic vocabulary so that they can better understand the words of Allah & enjoy their Salaah, inshaAllah.

This document lists all the words that appear in the Holy Qur'an.

Though there are a total of 77429 words in the Holy Qur'an, these can be reduced to 4845 words after removing all the duplicates, and various conjugations of the same word. Some words might appear twice if they have a different meaning. Some words might have the same root but are listed multiple times if they have a different grammatical context.

This work is not free of any mistakes, and is continuously being updated for corrections inshaAllah.

Please check http://quran.ilmsummit.org for updated versions of this file. You can also provide your comments, suggestions, corrections & questions on this site. Print this document in landscape mode.

May Allah accept this work & help us benefit from this work. Aameen.

Credits:
Corpus.quran.com
Openburhan.com

#	Word	Meaning	Frequency	Complete	Verse	Translation
1	مِنْ	from, of	3226	4.16%	مِن شَرِّ مَا خَلَقَ	"From the evil of what He has created; [Al-Falaq 113:2]
2	اللَّهُ	Allah	2699	7.65%	اللَّهُ الصَّمَدُ	"Allah-us-Samad (The Self-Sufficient Master, Whom all creatures need, He neither eats nor drinks). [Al-'Ikhlas 112:2]
3	لَا	No, not	2323	10.65%	كَلَّا لَا وَزَرَ	No! There is no refuge! [Al-Qiyamah 75:11]
4	فِي	in	1701	12.84%	فِي رَقٍّ مَّنشُورٍ	In parchment unrolled. [At-Tur 52:3]
5	إِنَّ	Indeed	1682	15.02%	إِنَّا لَمُغْرَمُونَ	(Saying): "We are indeed Mughramun (i.e. ruined or lost the money without any profit, or punished by the loss of all that we spend for cultivation, etc.)! [See Tafsir Al-Qurtubi, Vol. 17, Page 219] [Al-Waqi'ah 56:66]
6	قَالَ	to say	1618	17.11%	وَقِيلَ مَنْ رَاقٍ	And it will be said: "Who can cure him and save him from death?" [Al-Qiyamah 75:27]
7	الَّذِي	who, which, that	1465	19%	الَّذِي أَنقَضَ ظَهْرَكَ	Which weighed down your back? [Ash-Sharh 94:3]
8	عَلَى	On	1445	20.86%	عَلَيْهَا تِسْعَةَ عَشَرَ	Over it are nineteen (angels as guardians and keepers of Hell). [Al-Muddaththir 74:30]
9	لِ	For	1407	22.68%	مَا لَهُ مِن دَافِعٍ	There is none that can avert it; [At-Tur 52:8]
10	كَانَ	to be	1358	24.44%	وَإِن كَانُوا لَيَقُولُونَ	And indeed they (Arab pagans) used to say; [As-Saffat 37:167]
11	مَا	What	1174	25.95%	مَا الْحَاقَّةُ	What is the Reality? [Al-Haqqah 69:2]
12	رَبِّ	And your Lord	975	27.21%	وَرَبَّكَ فَكَبِّرْ	And your Lord (Allah) magnify! [Al-Muddaththir 74:3]
13	مَنْ	Who	824	28.28%	فَأَمَّا مَن طَغَى	Then, for him who Tagha (transgressed all bounds, in disbelief, oppression and evil deeds of disobedience to Allah). [An-Nazi'at 79:37]
14	بِ	with, by	819	29.33%	اشْدُدْ بِهِ أَزْرِي	"Increase my strength with him, [Taha 20:31]
15	إِلَى	to, toward, until	742	30.29%	إِلَى قَدَرٍ مَّعْلُومٍ	For a known period (determined by gestation)? [Al-Mursalat 77:22]
16	إِنْ	Not	694	31.19%	إِنْ أَنتَ إِلَّا نَذِيرٌ	You (O Muhammad SAW) are only a warner (i.e. your duty is to convey Allah's Message to mankind but the guidance is in Allah's Hand). [Fatir 35:23]
17	إِلَّا	Except	664	32.05%	إِلَّا الْمُصَلِّينَ	Except those devoted to Salat (prayers) [Al-Ma'arij 70:22]
18	أَنْ	That, to	613	32.84%	أَن رَّآهُ اسْتَغْنَى	Because he considers himself self-sufficient. [Al-'Alaq 96:7]
19	آمَنَ	to believe	537	33.53%	فَمَا لَهُمْ لَا يُؤْمِنُونَ	What is the matter with them, that they believe not? [Al-'Inshiqaq 84:20]
20	ذَلِكَ	That	479	34.15%	عُتُلٍّ بَعْدَ ذَلِكَ زَنِيمٍ	Cruel, after all that base-born (of illegitimate birth). [Al-Qalam 68:13]
21	عَنْ	From/about	465	34.75%	عَنِ الْمُجْرِمِينَ	About Al-Mujrimun (polytheists, criminals, disbelievers, etc.), (And they will say to them): [Al-Muddaththir 74:41]
22	هُوَ	He	464	35.35%	وَهُوَ يَخْشَى	And is afraid (of Allah and His Punishment), ['Abasa 80:9]
23	أَرْضِ	the Earth, land	461	35.94%	وَإِذَا الْأَرْضُ مُدَّتْ	And when the earth is stretched forth, [Al-'Inshiqaq 84:3]
24	إِذَا	when	423	36.49%	عَبْدًا إِذَا صَلَّى	A slave (Muhammad (Peace be upon him)) when he prays? [Al-'Alaq 96:10]
25	قَدْ	Indeed	406	37.01%	وَقَدْ خَابَ مَن دَسَّاهَا	And indeed he fails who corrupts his ownself (i.e. disobeys what Allah has ordered by rejecting the true Faith of Islamic Monotheism or by following polytheism, etc. or by doing every kind of evil wicked deeds). [Ash-Shams 91:10]

No.	Word	Meaning	Count	%	Example	Translation
26	يَوْم	For a Day	405	37.54%	يَوْمٍ عَظِيم	On a Great Day, [Al-Mutaffifin 83:5]
27	قَوْم	(the) people	383	38.03%	كَذَّبَتْ قَوْمُ لُوطٍ بِالنُّذُر	The people of Lout (Lot) belied the warnings. [Al-Qamar 54:33]
28	آيَة	the sign	382	38.53%	فَأَرَاهُ الآيَةَ الكُبْرَى	Then [Musa (Moses)] showed him the great sign (miracles). [An-Nazi'at 79:20]
29	عَلِمَ	to know	382	39.02%	كَلَّا سَيَعْلَمُون	Nay, they will come to know! [An-Naba' 78:4]
30	هُمْ	They	370	39.5%	الَّذِينَ هُمْ يُرَاءُون	Those who do good deeds only to be seen (of men), [Al-Ma'un 107:6]
31	أَنَّ	That	366	39.97%	وَظَنَّ أَنَّهُ الفِرَاق	And he (the dying person) will conclude that it was (the time) of departing (death); [Al-Qiyamah 75:28]
32	كُلّ	Everyone	359	40.43%	كُلُّ مَنْ عَلَيْهَا فَانٍ	Whatsoever is on it (the earth) will perish. [Ar-Rahman 55:26]
33	لَمْ	Not	348	40.88%	لَمْ يَلِدْ وَلَمْ يُولَدْ	"He begets not, nor was He begotten; [Al-'Ikhlas 112:3]
34	ثُمَّ	Then	341	41.32%	ثُمَّ نَظَر	Then he thought; [Al-Muddaththir 74:21]
35	جَعَلَ	to make	340	41.76%	فَجَعَلَهُ غُثَاءً أَحْوَى	And then makes it dark stubble. [Al-'A'la 87:5]
36	رَسُول	the Messengers	332	42.19%	وَإِذَا الرُّسُلُ أُقِّتَت	And when the Messengers are gathered to their time appointed; [Al-Mursalat 77:11]
37	عَذَاب	My punishment	322	42.61%	فَذُوقُوا عَذَابِي وَنُذُر	"Then taste you My Torment and My Warnings." [Al-Qamar 54:39]
38	سَمَاء	By the sky	310	43.01%	وَالسَّمَاءِ وَالطَّارِق	By the heaven, and At-Tariq (the night-comer, i.e. the bright star); [At-Tariq 86:1]
39	نَفْس	self, soul, person, mind	295	43.39%	وَنَفْسٍ وَمَا سَوَّاهَا	And by Nafs (Adam or a person or a soul, etc.), and Him Who perfected him in proportion; [Ash-Shams 91:7]
40	كَفَرَ	to disbelieve	289	43.76%	إِلَّا مَنْ تَوَلَّى وَكَفَر	Save the one who turns away and disbelieves [Al-Ghashiyah 88:23]
41	شَيْء	thing	283	44.13%	مِنْ أَيِّ شَيْءٍ خَلَقَه	From what thing did He create him? ['Abasa 80:18]
42	أَوْ	Or	280	44.49%	عُذْرًا أَوْ نُذْرًا	To cut off all excuses or to warn; [Al-Mursalat 77:6]
43	جَاءَ	to come	278	44.85%	أَنْ جَاءَهُ الأَعْمَى	Because there came to him the blind man (i.e. 'Abdullah bin Umm-Maktum, who came to the Prophet (Peace be upon him) while he was preaching to one or some of the Quraish chiefs). ['Abasa 80:2]
44	عَمِلَ	to do, to work	276	45.2%	عَمَّا كَانُوا يَعْمَلُون	For all that they used to do. [Al-Hijr 15:93]
45	لَوْ	If	276	45.56%	وَلَوْ أَلْقَى مَعَاذِيرَه	Though he may put forth his excuses (to cover his evil deeds). [Al-Qiyamah 75:15]
46	هَذَا	This	274	45.91%	هَذَا يَوْمُ لَا يَنْطِقُون	That will be a Day when they shall not speak (during some part of it), [Al-Mursalat 77:35]
47	أَتَى	to give	271	46.26%	الَّذِي يُؤْتِي مَالَهُ يَتَزَكَّى	He who spends his wealth for increase in self-purification, [Al-Layl 92:18]
48	رَأَى	to see	271	46.61%	وَنَرَاهُ قَرِيبًا	But We see it (quite) near. [Al-Ma'arij 70:7]
49	بَيْن	Between both of them	266	46.96%	بَيْنَهُمَا بَرْزَخٌ لَا يَبْغِيَان	Between them is a barrier which none of them can transgress. [Ar-Rahman 55:20]
50	أَتَى	to come, to bring	264	47.3%	حَتَّى أَتَانَا اليَقِين	"Until there came to us (the death) that is certain." [Al-Muddaththir 74:47]
51	كِتَاب	A book	260	47.63%	كِتَابٌ مَرْقُوم	A Register inscribed. [Al-Mutaffifin 83:20]
52	حَقّ	surely (the) truth	247	47.95%	وَإِنَّهُ لَحَقُّ اليَقِين	And Verily, it (this Quran) is an absolute truth with certainty. [Al-Haqqah 69:51]
53	قَبْل	before	242	48.27%	إِنَّهُمْ كَانُوا قَبْلَ ذَلِكَ مُتْرَفِين	Verily, before that, they indulged in luxury, [Al-Waqi'ah 56:45]

#	Arabic	Meaning	Count	%	Example	Translation
54	نَاسٍ	(of) mankind	241	48.58%	مَلِكِ النَّاسِ	"The King of mankind, [An-Nas 114:2]
55	إِذْ	when	239	48.89%	إِذِ انبَعَثَ أَشْقَاهَا	When the most wicked man among them went forth (to kill the she-camel). [Ash-Shams 91:12]
56	شَاءَ	to will, to wish	236	49.19%	فَمَن شَاءَ ذَكَرَهُ	So whoever wills, let him pay attention to it. [Abasa 80:12]
57	أُوْلَٰئِكَ	Those	208	49.46%	أُوْلَٰئِكَ الْمُقَرَّبُونَ	These will be those nearest to Allah. [Al-Waqi'ah 56:11]
58	مُؤْمِن	(are) the believers	202	49.72%	قَدْ أَفْلَحَ الْمُؤْمِنُونَ	Successful indeed are the believers. [Al-Mu'minun 23:1]
59	بَعْد	after	199	49.98%	عُتُلٍّ بَعْدَ ذَٰلِكَ زَنِيمٍ	Cruel, after all that base-born (of illegitimate birth), [Al-Qalam 68:13]
60	عِنْد	Near	197	50.23%	عِندَ سِدْرَةِ الْمُنتَهَىٰ	Near Sidrat-ul-Muntaha [lote-tree of the utmost boundary (beyond which none can pass)]. [An-Najm 53:14]
61	خَلَقَ	to create	184	50.47%	خَلَقَ الْإِنسَانَ	He created man. [Ar-Rahman 55:3]
62	أَنزَلَ	to send down, to reveal	183	50.71%	كَمَا أَنزَلْنَا عَلَى الْمُقْتَسِمِينَ	As We have sent down on the dividers, (Quraish pagans or Jews and Christians). [Al-Hijr 15:90]
63	خَيْر	(is) better	178	50.94%	وَالْآخِرَةُ خَيْرٌ وَأَبْقَىٰ	Although the Hereafter is better and more lasting. [Al-A'la 87:17]
64	سَبِيل	the way	176	51.16%	ثُمَّ السَّبِيلَ يَسَّرَهُ	Then He makes the Path easy for him; [Abasa 80:20]
65	كَذَّبَ	to deny, to reject	176	51.39%	فَكَذَّبَ وَعَصَىٰ	But [Fir'aun (Pharaoh)] belied and disobeyed; [An-Nazi'at 79:21]
66	دَعَا	to call, to invite, to pray	170	51.61%	فَلْيَدْعُ نَادِيَهُ	Then, let him call upon his council (of helpers), [Al-'Alaq 96:17]
67	أَمْر	command, affair, matter	166	51.82%	وَيَسِّرْ لِي أَمْرِي	"And ease my task for me; [Taha 20:26]
68	اتَّقَىٰ	to be righteous, to fear (Allah)	166	52.04%	فَاتَّقُوا اللَّهَ وَأَطِيعُونِ	"So fear Allah, keep your duty to Him, and obey me. [Ash-Shu'ara' 26:144]
69	لَمَّا	When/then	165	52.25%	كَلَّا لَمَّا يَقْضِ مَا أَمَرَهُ	Nay, but (man) has not done what He commanded him. [Abasa 80:23]
70	مَعَ	With	164	52.46%	إِنَّ مَعَ الْعُسْرِ يُسْرًا	Verily, with the hardship, there is relief (i.e. there is one hardship with two reliefs, so one hardship cannot overcome two reliefs). [Ash-Sharh 94:6]
71	عَلِيم	learned	163	52.67%	يَأْتُوكَ بِكُلِّ سَاحِرٍ عَلِيمٍ	"That they bring up to you all well-versed sorcerers." [Al-A'raf 7:112]
72	يَبْعَض	some	157	52.88%	وَلَوْ تَقَوَّلَ عَلَيْنَا بَعْضَ الْأَقَاوِيلِ	And if he (Muhammad SAW) had forged a false saying concerning Us (Allah), [Al-Haqqah 69:44]
73	آخَر	Hereafter, end, last, later generations	155	53.08%	وَتَذَرُونَ الْآخِرَةَ	And leave (neglect) the Hereafter. [Al-Qiyamah 75:21]
74	إِلَٰه	god	147	53.27%	إِلَٰهِ النَّاسِ	"The Ilah (God) of mankind, [An-Nas 114:3]
75	جَنَّة	My Paradise	147	53.46%	وَادْخُلِي جَنَّتِي	"And enter you My Paradise!" [Al-Fajr 89:30]
76	غَيْر	not	147	53.65%	عَلَى الْكَافِرِينَ غَيْرُ يَسِيرٍ	Far from easy for the disbelievers. [Al-Muddaththir 74:10]
77	نَار	A Fire	145	53.83%	نَارٌ حَامِيَةٌ	(It is) a hot blazing Fire! [Al-Qari'ah 101:11]
78	دُون	Besides these two	144	54.02%	وَمِن دُونِهِمَا جَنَّتَانِ	And besides these two, there are two other Gardens (i.e. in Paradise). [Ar-Rahman 55:62]
79	هَدَىٰ	to guide	144	54.21%	وَالَّذِي قَدَّرَ فَهَدَىٰ	And Who has measured (preordainments for each and everything even to be blessed or wretched); then guided (i.e. showed mankind the right as well as wrong paths, and guided the animals to pasture); [Al-A'la 87:3]
80	أَيُّهَا	O	143	54.39%	يَا أَيُّهَا الْمُدَّثِّرُ	O you (Muhammad SAW) enveloped (in garments)! [Al-Muddaththir 74:1]